GAME ON!

THE LEGEND OF ZELDA

LUNA THOMAS

Checkerboard
Library

An Imprint of Abdo Publishing
abdobooks.com

abdobooks.com

Published by Abdo Publishing, a division of ABDO, PO Box 398166, Minneapolis, Minnesota 55439. Copyright © 2022 by Abdo Consulting Group, Inc. International copyrights reserved in all countries. No part of this book may be reproduced in any form without written permission from the publisher. Checkerboard Library™ is a trademark and logo of Abdo Publishing.

Printed in the United States of America, North Mankato, Minnesota
052021
092021

THIS BOOK CONTAINS
RECYCLED MATERIALS

Design: Aruna Rangarajan, Mighty Media, Inc.
Production: Mighty Media, Inc.
Editor: Rebecca Felix
Design Elements: Shutterstock Images
Cover Photograph: tofoli.douglas/Flickr
Interior Photographs: Ali Mohammed/Wikimedia Commons, p. 13; ArcadeImages /Alamy, p. 24 (left); Brett Chalupa/ Flickr, p. 23; Chris Pizzello/AP Images, pp. 7, 28 (bottom); Colony of Gamers/Flickr, p. 5; Evan Amos/Vanamo Media/ Wikimedia Commons, p. 24; Flavio Dechen/Flickr, p. 11, 28; Gilles BASSIGNAC/Getty Images, p. 21; Instacodez/Flickr, p. 15; Javi G Ch/Flickr, p. 25 (top); Johan Larsson/Flickr, p. 8; Justin Evans/Flickr, p. 9; The Pop Culture Geek Network/ Flickr, pp. 27, 29; Sara Reis/Flickr, p. 19; Shutterstock Images, pp. 25, 29 (top); Simon Starr/Flickr, p. 17; slgckgc/Flickr, p. 12

Library of Congress Control Number: 2020949738

Publisher's Cataloging-in-Publication Data
Names: Thomas, Luna, author.
Title: The Legend of Zelda / by Luna Thomas
Description: Minneapolis, Minnesota : Abdo Publishing, 2022 | Series: Game On! | Includes online resources and index.
Identifiers: ISBN 9781532195792 (lib. bdg.) | ISBN 9781644945513 (pbk.) | ISBN 9781098216528 (ebook)
Subjects: LCSH: Video games--Juvenile literature. | Legend of Zelda (Game)--Juvenile literature. | Nintendo video games--Juvenile literature. | Fantasy games--Juvenile literature. | Video games and children--Juvenile literature.
Classification: DDC 794.8--dc2

NOTE TO READERS

Video games that depict shooting or other violent acts should be subject to adult discretion and awareness that exposure to such acts may affect players' perceptions of violence in the real world.

CONTENTS

A LASTING LEGEND

A young boy with pointed ears and a magic sword runs across an open field. Ahead of him lies a crystal blue lake. To the west lies a **vast** desert. A dark forest stands to the south. A range of mountains rises to the east. Where should the boy explore first? It's up to the player to decide!

The Legend of Zelda is a world-famous video game. It follows the adventures of a boy named Link. Players guide Link through the fantasy world of Hyrule as he works to complete a **quest**. This quest is often to save the Princess Zelda from an evil villain.

The *Zelda* **franchise** is one of the most popular game series of all time. Millions of *Zelda* games have been sold since the first one launched more than 30 years ago. New games are still being made. And fans have only become more excited by the ever-growing kingdom of Hyrule and Link's missions within it.

Link in *The Legend of Zelda: Skyward Sword*. The 2011 game explained the origins of the Master Sword. Link uses this weapon in many games in the series.

RECREATING ADVENTURE

The Legend of Zelda's creator is Shigeru Miyamoto. As a child, Miyamoto loved to explore the countryside around his home in Sonobe, Japan. He hiked through forests and explored caves. Miyamoto grew up to be a video game designer. In 1977, he began working for the company Nintendo. But he never forgot his childhood adventures.

At Nintendo, Miyamoto's job was to come up with new game ideas. By 1985, he had helped design several games, including *Donkey Kong* and *Super Mario Bros.*

In these games, players were guided through levels where they tried to score as many points as possible. Defeating enemies or completing tasks earned players points. By completing enough

MIYAMOTO'S CAVE

When asked about what inspired *Zelda*, Miyamoto says when he was around eight years old, he discovered a hole in the ground. Miyamoto returned later with a lantern and crawled into the hole. He was in a cave! Miyamoto spent the summer exploring the cave.

tasks, players moved on to the next level.

These points-based games were popular. But they were also highly structured. Players could only move through a game in one way. Miyamoto wanted to try something different.

Fantasy was not a popular video game genre when Shigeru Miyamoto was creating *Zelda*. Because of this, Miyamoto didn't believe his game would become popular. But gamers loved it!

BUILDING A WORLD

In 1984, Miyamoto got the opportunity to turn his vision for an adventure game into reality. Nintendo had recently released its Famicom game **console**. And Miyamoto was charged with designing a new game for it.

Other video games at the time required players to move along a **predetermined** path. Miyamoto wanted his game to give players the freedom to explore. He was inspired by role-playing games (RPGs). These were a popular type of tabletop board game that involved journeying through mythical worlds.

Miyamoto began work on a **prototype**. In it, two players built dungeons and could then explore each other's creations. When testing the game, Miyamoto and his team

HYRULE

Each game in the *Zelda* **franchise** explored a different part of Hyrule's history. The book *Hyrule Historia* gives the full story of Hyrule's timeline.

HYRULE HISTORIA

ZELDA

Hyrule included features of the Japanese countryside Miyamoto explored as a child. But the final world looked more like medieval Europe.

decided the exploration was the funnest part. So, they focused on building a whole world for players to explore. The world became known as Hyrule.

CODING ADVENTURE

Creating a player-directed game presented **coding** challenges. Every possible action a *Zelda* player might take would need to be coded into the game. Fortunately, new developments in technology made such coding possible.

Early **consoles** had certain games built into their hardware. But Famicom's games were sold as disks separate from the consoles. Disk-based consoles had four times as much memory as previous consoles. This allowed the developers to create more **complex** games.

Zelda was originally produced on floppy disks. The data on the disks could be rewritten as a player played the game. Players could save their progress and pick up where they left off the next time

LOADING...

Zelda's developers had to consider many features. For example, they knew players would be frustrated while waiting for game elements to load. So, they had the elements load during natural game **transitions**, such as characters climbing a staircase.

The Legend of Zelda was sold on floppy disks in Japan.
In the United States, it was sold on gold game cartridges.

they played. *Zelda* was the first game to have a save feature
backed by a battery, creating an entirely new style of gameplay.

A FRANCHISE IS BORN

Nintendo **debuted** *The Legend of Zelda* in Japan for the Famicom on February 21, 1986. The game's US release was August 22, 1987, on the Nintendo Entertainment System (NES) **console**.

Zelda's mythical world of Hyrule featured **2D** dungeons and forests. Compared to other games released at the time, *Zelda*'s **graphics** were simple. But the gameplay was **complex**.

PRINCESS ZELDA

Zelda appears in all *Zelda* games. In many, Link is tasked with rescuing her. In others, Zelda acts as a hero!

A Zelda figurine

THE LEGEND OF ZELDA

©1986 NINTENDO

PUSH START BUTTON

Zelda was the first video game that allowed players to save their progress. Previous games reset each time their console was powered down.

Players navigated the game from an overhead view. Playing as Link, gamers completed a **quest** to rescue the princess Zelda from a villain, later named Ganon.

Zelda required players to read sections of text to follow the story. Nintendo staff worried American gamers would not like this. But the game was a smash hit!

AN INSTANT HIT

Players loved *Zelda.* It became the first stand-alone Nintendo game in history to sell 1 million copies! By 2020, it would sell almost 7 million copies worldwide. The first game's success paved the way for *Zelda* games that followed.

In 1992, Nintendo released *The Legend of Zelda: A Link to the Past* in the United States. The game was created for the Super Nintendo Entertainment System (SNES).

A Link to the Past introduced players to the concept of parallel worlds. In the game, Link traveled between a light **realm** and a dark realm. This would become a common feature in the **franchise's** future games.

In 1993, Nintendo released *The Legend of Zelda: Link's Awakening* for its handheld Game Boy **console**. *Zelda* fans could now play on the go! And *Zelda* would soon enter another new gaming realm to great success.

THE LEGEND OF ZELDA™
Link's Awakening

Link's Awakening took place on Hyrule's Koholint Island. It was the first *Zelda* game to include a fishing minigame. Almost every *Zelda* game since has featured a fishing minigame like it.

ZELDA GOES 3D

Throughout the 1980s and 1990s, computer and TV **graphics** were limited. So, many video games from this era used **2D** graphics, including the first few *Zelda* games.

The technology for **3D** video games had been around since the early 1980s. But video game hardware was not advanced enough to present 3D graphics well. Many early 3D graphics looked overly simple and awkward.

Over the years, 3D technology improved. In 1998, Nintendo released *The Legend of Zelda: Ocarina of Time* for the Nintendo 64 **console**. For the first time, *Zelda*'s world was in 3D.

Ocarina of Time sold 2 million copies in its first 39 days! It pushed the boundaries of what players expected from video games. Many modern gamers still consider it one of the best video games of all time.

ZELDA ON TV

In 1989, *The Legend of Zelda* TV series ran from September to December in the United States. However, the show received poor reviews, so only 13 episodes were made.

MADE IN JAPAN

Original
Nintendo
Seal of
Quality

THIS SEAL IS YOUR ASSURANCE
THAT NINTENDO HAS APPROVED
THE QUALITY OF THIS PRODUCT.
ALWAYS LOOK FOR THIS SEAL
WHEN BUYING GAMES AND
ACCESSORIES TO ENSURE COM-
PLETE COMPATIBILITY WITH YOUR
NINTENDO 64.

IMPORTANT!
Please read the precaution booklet
inside.

**FOR USE WITH PAL VERSION
NINTENDO 64 ONLY.**

**NOT COMPATIBLE WITH JA-
PANESE AND U.S. VERSION
NINTENDO 64 CONTROL DECK.**

**CONTAINS ENGLISH, SWEDISH,
DANISH AND FINNISH LANGUAGE
INSTRUCTION.**

WARRANTY
WARRANTY PROVIDED (Complete
warranty information inside box)
WARRANTY VALID ONLY IN THE
U.K., EIRE. FOR SCANDINAVIA
MARKET, PLEASE CONTACT TO
BERGSALA AB.

For Ages – Pour Ages – Para Años – Für Jahre – Per Anni

| 3-10 | ✓ | 11-14 | ✓ |
| 15-17 | ✓ | 18+ | ✓ |

ELSPA

COPYRIGHT (C) 1994, EUROPEAN LEISURE SOFTWARE
PUBLISHERS ASSOCIATION. ALL RIGHTS RESERVED.

This product is exempt from classification under U.K.Law
In accordance with The Video Standards Council Code of Practice
it is considered suitable for viewing by the age range(s) indicated.

NUS-006 (-01.) (EUR)

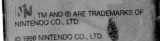
TM AND ® ARE TRADEMARKS OF
NINTENDO CO., LTD.
© 1998 NINTENDO CO., LTD.

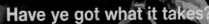

Nin

Have ye got what it takes?

An epic adventure beyond your wildest dreams,
Shigeru Miyamoto's latest masterpiece is an
incredible gaming experience, like nothing you
have ever seen before. Descend into the for-
bidden dungeons of Hyrule and use ancient clues
and secret passages to clear your way closer to
the heart, and the monstrous guardians which
lurk for you there. Epic gameplay deeply immerses
you into the unfolding storyline, and breathtaking
realtime visual effects will transport you into a
fantastic world full of mysteries, secrets and terri-
fying legends. An incredible interactive environ-
ment allows you to fight your way through hordes
of Ganon's evil minions, dabble in the mystic arts
and ride across barren plains on horseback…

- The latest instalment in Shigeru Miyamoto's classic adventure series
- 256 megs of intensive action-adventure gaming
- Incredible visuals and a powerful orchestral soundtrack
- Game progress is saved to the cartridge
- Rumble Pak compatibility helps you seek out hidden treasures and secrets!

NUS-P-NZLP-N

0 45496 87000

Ocarina of Time's packaging gave glimpses of its 3D gameplay
and challenged players, "Have ye got what it takes?"

CHARACTER DEVELOPMENT

The real magic behind the *Zelda* games has always been the characters and settings. Since 1992, illustrator Yusuke Nakano has brought these elements to life. He has been involved in the illustration for nine *Zelda* games.

All *Zelda* games feature some of Miyamoto's original characters. But the characters change a bit in each one. In some, Link is a boy. In others, he is a teenager or adult. New characters and Hyrule settings are also introduced in each game.

Nakano develops concept art for each game he illustrates. These are sketches of characters from different views. Other developers review the sketches and give feedback.

Nakano considers the plot of the game when designing characters. In *The Legend of Zelda: Twilight Princess*, Link has the power to turn into a wolf. So, Nakano gave him wolflike eyes and a wild haircut in that game. The character's appearance added to the look and feel of the story.

THE LEGEND OF

ELDA

OCARINA OF TIME

LINK

arina of Time, Link's shield, inset with
crest, has been treated symbolically.
now stand proud and tall, completely
d by its weight. His long ears, a charac-
f the Hylia, are also further emphasized.

Child Link

THE LEGEND CONTINUES

Miyamoto only directed the first *Zelda* game. But he stayed on as **producer**, overseeing the work of other directors. Between 2000 and 2020, Nintendo released more than 10 *Zelda* games. These games had new **quests** and characters but stayed true to Miyamoto's original vision.

In 2004, the **franchise** released its first multiplayer game, *The Legend of Zelda: Four Swords*. Up to four players could play the game together. *Four Swords* was popular. But its **console**, Nintendo's GameCube, was discontinued a few years later.

In 2006, Nintendo launched its Wii console and a *Zelda* game to play on it. *The Legend of Zelda: Twilight Princess* used gesture-based controls. This allowed players to control *Zelda* characters in a whole new way.

GUEST STAR

Link has appeared in other Nintendo games. In 1999, he was a character in *Super Smash Bros*. In 2003, he appeared in *Soulcalibur II*. And in 2014, he was a racer in *Mario Kart*.

A gamer uses both the Wii Nunchuck (*left*) and Wiimote (*right*) motion-capture controllers to play *Twilight Princess*.

A BREATH OF FRESH AIR

Between 2011 and 2015, the *Zelda* **franchise** released three new games. These were *Skyward Sword* in 2011, *A Link Between Worlds* in 2013, and *Tri Force Heroes* in 2015. Reviewers complained about the games' poor design and awkward motion controls. It seemed that *Zelda* had lost its way.

In 2017, *Zelda* released *The Legend of Zelda: Breath of the Wild* on both the Wii U and Nintendo's handheld Switch **console**. In the game, Link could go anywhere the player chose right from the start. Skilled players could even choose to go straight to the game's final battle without completing side **quests**.

Breath of the Wild also featured sweeping landscapes and beautiful settings captured extremely well in the game's **graphics**. Many reviewers called it the best game of the *Zelda* franchise. Fans also loved *Breath of the Wild*. By fall of 2020, it had sold more than 20 million copies. This made it the best-selling *Zelda* game of all time!

In *Breath of the Wild*, Link's journey began on a geographical feature called the Great Plateau.

THE LEGEND OF
ZELDA
BREATH OF THE WILD

LEVEL UP!

Zelda: Ongoing Quests

No matter the version, *Zelda* is a game of **quests** and puzzles. In each game, Link's quest is to save Hyrule and defeat evil. Along the way, he can complete side quests and collect different weapons and tools.

Hyrule is made up of two main regions. These are the underworld and overworld. Link spends much time exploring the overworld. But many of his battles take place in the underworld. It has different dungeons, each protected by a guardian known as a boss. When Link defeats a boss, he will usually win an item. This allows him to continue his quest.

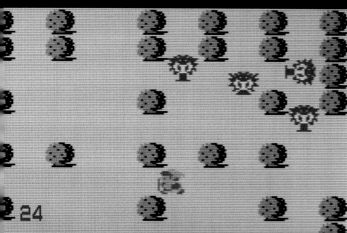

1986 (Japan), **1987** (US)

THE LEGEND OF ZELDA

+ **Consoles**: Famicom (Japan) and Nintendo Entertainment System (US)

+ Main Quest: Rescue the kidnapped princess Zelda from Ganon

+ **2D**

+ Single player

+ 9 Dungeons

+ Fun fact: Features a more challenging second quest after the main quest is completed

Famicom is short for "Family Computer."

THE LEGEND OF ZELDA: BREATH OF THE WILD

+ **Consoles**: Nintendo Wii U and Nintendo Switch

+ Main **Quest**: Defeat Ganon and save Hyrule

+ **3D** and virtual reality

+ Single player

+ 120 shrines (which serve as mini dungeons)

+ Fun fact: Players can move through the game in any way they choose, including attempting to complete the final challenge before completing any side quest.

Nintendo Switch controllers could be used three ways. They could be attached to the console, used as a remote for the console, or used as a remote for a TV or computer screen.

ZELDA FOREVER

The *Zelda* **franchise** has continued to thrive and expand. For years, there were rumors of *Zelda* movies and TV series being developed. Fans eagerly awaited confirmation whether these rumors were true.

Meanwhile, the music of *Zelda* had also found an audience. In 2011, three concerts celebrated *Zelda*'s twenty-fifth anniversary. In 2012, these concerts became a tour called The Symphony of the Goddess. The popular tour traveled the world for five years.

In the gaming **realm**, Nintendo released **updated** versions of older *Zelda* games. This allowed them to be played on newer **consoles**.

In 2019, Nintendo released a trailer for a *Breath of the Wild* **sequel**. But the release date remained unknown. Fans hoped for new content soon. No matter what would come next for *Zelda*, the legend was far from over.

A 2011 concert celebrating *Zelda*'s twenty-fifth anniversary. Koji Kondo is the composer who creates the music of *Zelda*. He is also known for composing the music to other popular video games, including *Super Mario Bros*.

TIMELINE

1986

On February 21, Nintendo releases *The Legend of Zelda* in Japan.

1992

Nintendo releases *The Legend of Zelda: A Link to the Past* in the United States.

1977

Shigeru Miyamoto begins working for Nintendo.

1987

Nintendo releases *The Legend of Zelda* in the United States on August 22.

1993

Nintendo releases its first *Zelda* game for a handheld console, *The Legend of Zelda: Link's Awakening*.

1998

Nintendo releases its first 3D *Zelda* game, *The Legend of Zelda: Ocarina of Time.*

2006

Nintendo releases *The Legend of Zelda: Twilight Princess.*

2017

Nintendo releases *The Legend of Zelda: Breath of the Wild.* It becomes the best-selling *Zelda* game of all time.

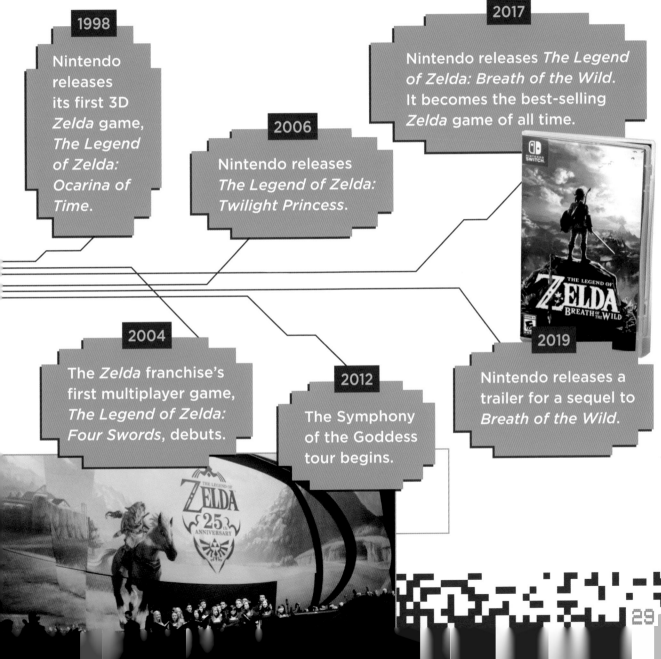

2004

The *Zelda* franchise's first multiplayer game, *The Legend of Zelda: Four Swords*, debuts.

2012

The Symphony of the Goddess tour begins.

2019

Nintendo releases a trailer for a sequel to *Breath of the Wild.*

GLOSSARY

code—a set of instructions for a computer to run a program.

complex—having many parts, details, ideas, or functions.

console—an electronic system used to play video games.

debut (DAY-byoo)—to first appear.

franchise—a series of related works, such as movies or video games, that feature the same characters.

graphics—images on the screen of a computer, TV, or other device.

predetermined—something that is determined beforehand.

producer—a person who oversees or provides money for a play, TV show, movie, album, or video game.

prototype—an early model of a product on which future versions can be modeled.

quest—a long journey in search of something or to complete a task.

realm—a domain, kingdom, or area of activity.

sequel—a movie, game, or other work that continues the story of a previous work.

3D—having length, width, and depth, or appearing to have these dimensions. *3D* stands for "three-dimensional."

transition—movement or development from one state, stage, or style to another.

2D—having length and width, but lacking the appearance of depth. *2D* stands for "two-dimensional."

update—to make something more modern or up-to-date.

vast—very great in size or amount.

ONLINE RESOURCES

Booklinks
NONFICTION NETWORK
FREE! ONLINE NONFICTION RESOURCES

To learn more about *The Legend of Zelda*, please visit **abdobooklinks.com** or scan this QR code. These links are routinely monitored and updated to provide the most current information available.

INDEX